MOM'S SUPERHERO

WRITTEN BY SANIYA CHITALE

ILLUSTRATED BY DHWANI GOSALIA

Ayan loves his mommy the mostest. When mommy smiles at him, calls him her peach, Ayan feels the happiest.

Mummy wakes up early every day
to prepare Ayan's breakfast.
She keeps the home spick-and-span
and tends to their beautiful garden.

Mummy does all this
and so much more.

She makes time for her research work and takes care of Ayan staying at home. Mummy is a superhero for Ayan.
She rarely seems to take a break.

She loves reading him story books right before bedtime.
Ayan is happy to be with Mummy and see her finally catch a break.

On a warm Monday morning Mrs Kapoor, the class teacher, declares,"Everyone should make time for something they love - - we call this a hobby."

"No matter how busy,
you must make time.
Draw, swim or read,
pick up a thing you like."

The children open their notebooks and write down their hobbies. Ayan jots down : swimming and tennis.

Virat puts down singing as his hobby. While Raj excitedly notes cooking and reading as his hobbies.

"Now moving on let's open our notebooks and write five new words," Mrs Kapoor calls out. Soon the bell rings and school is off.

Ayan, Raj and Virat decide
to play hide-and-seek.
Ayan's home is where
they plan to meet.

The game is so much fun. Ayan and Raj now decide to hide.

Ayan paces back and forth, unsure what to hide behind. His face lights up as soon as the idea strikes.

The old storage room will be the perfect place!

Ayan is confident, it would be impossible for Virat to trace.

Ayan hides behind an old cupboard as something drops hard. He finds atop the cupboard 20 cardboard boxes, all wrapped up in black cloth.

He stretches his arms, tries to open the boxes and peep.
But they are too high up and he can barely reach.

Ayan waits for Daddy to come home and asks him about the hidden box.

Ayan leads him to the storage room. Daddy is at a loss.

Daddy gets the boxes down and swishes them open.
He loudly exclaims, "Ah! That's where she hid those paintings!"
Ayan is confused.

"Whose paintings are those?" he asks.
"Your mummy's! She loved painting and won prizes galore," Daddy retorts.

Ayan is surprised as he looks at the paintings.

His Mummy never told him how much she loved painting.

"Why doesn't she
paint anymore?"
Ayan asks Daddy.
Why would Mummy
not tell him this,
Ayan feels sad
and weary.

"Don't feel bad, son.
Mummy just cannot find the time."
Something in his voice tells
Ayan that Daddy too is sad.

Next day after school, Ayan quickly tidies up his room and the living room.

He even places some flowers in the vase and puts things back in their place.

Mummy is surprised.
"Wow is this my lucky day? What is going on?" She asks with a broad smile on her face.

Ayan beams a dimpled, toothy smile at Mummy, holds her hand and says, "Mummy I am making time for your hobby – I know you love painting."

"Mrs Kapoor says we must find time for the things we love to do. I swim and play tennis, and daddy plays golf and football too."

"But you never find time for the one thing that you love." Mummy's eyes became teary, she kisses Ayan's forehead and wraps him in a hug.

"Thank you my angel for reminding me, the joy I feel when brushes and paints are all around me."

"You are my superhero." Mummy tells Ayan and pulls him close. That's the best thing Mummy has ever called him. He plants a peck on her nose.

Now Mummy paints every night after having dinner. Daddy and Ayan make sure they help out so she gets time for painting.

Mummy looks happier than ever, but Ayan is the happiest.